NEIL YOUNG
ANTHOLOGY EASY GUITAR

HEY HEY, MY MY
(INTO THE BLACK)

Words and Music by
NEIL YOUNG

Medium Rock beat

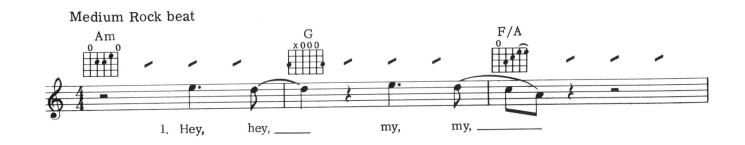

1. Hey, hey, _____ my, my, _____

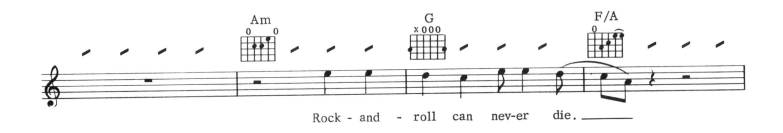

Rock - and - roll can nev-er die. _____

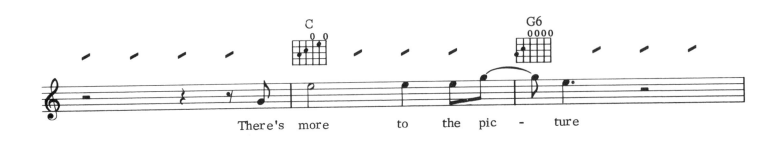

There's more to the pic - ture

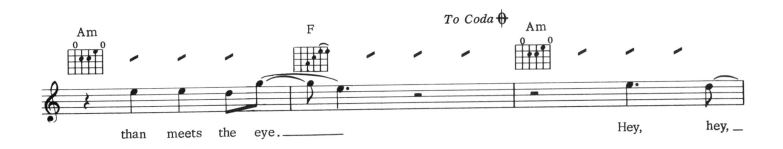

than meets the eye. _____ Hey, hey, —

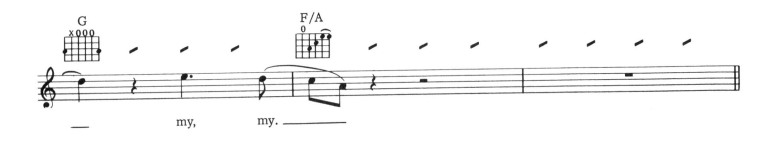

— my, my. _____

FOUR STRONG WINDS

Words and Music by
IAN TYSON

DOWN BY THE RIVER

Words and Music by
NEIL YOUNG

Be on my side, I'll be on your side,
You take my hand, I'll take_ your hand;_

_ ba - by; there is no rea - son for
to - geth - er we may get a-

you to hide._
way. It's so hard for me
This much mad - ness is

stay - in' here all a - lone,_ when you could
too much sor - row;_ it's im -

be tak - in' me for a ride,_
pos - si - ble to make it to - day,

yeah, yeah._ She could
yeah, yeah._

drag me o - ver the rain - bow_ and

ARE YOU READY FOR THE COUNTRY?

Words and Music by
NEIL YOUNG

Moderately

1. Slip-pin' and a - slid-in' and play-in' dom - i - nos,
talk-in' to the preach-er said God was on my side,
then I

left-in' and then right-in', it's not a crime you know.
ran in-to the hang-man, he said,"It's time to die."
You
You

got-ta tell your sto-ry, boy, be-fore it's time to go.
got-ta tell your sto-ry, boy, you know the rea-son why.
Are you

read-y for the coun-try, be-cause it's time to go?
Are you

read-y for the coun-try, be-cause it's time to go?

1.

2.

2. I was

COUNTRY GIRL

Words and Music by
NEIL YOUNG

Coda

Find out that now was the an-swer to an-swers that you gave lat-er. She did the things that we both did be-fore now, but who for-gave her? If I could stand to see her cry-ing I would tell her not to care. When she learns of all your ly-ing will she join you there.

Repeat and fade

Coun-try girl, I think you're pret-ty; got to make you un-der-stand.
Have no lov-ers in the cit-y; let me be your coun-try man.

HELPLESS

Words and Music by
NEIL YOUNG

Moderately slow

There is a town in north On - tar - i - o

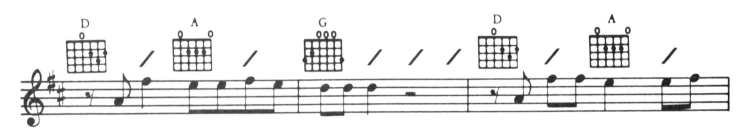

with dream com-fort mem-o - ry to spare;   and in my mind   I still

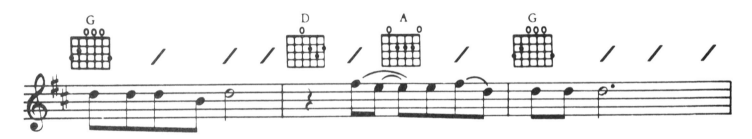

need a place to go,   all___ my chang - es were there.

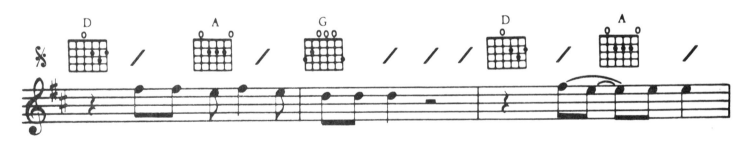

Blue, blue win-dows be - hind the stars,   yel - low moon

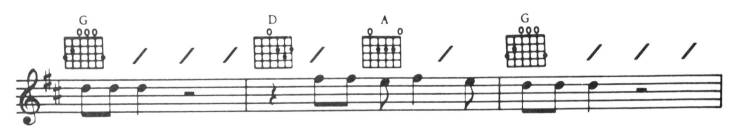

on the rise;   big birds fly - ing a - cross the sky

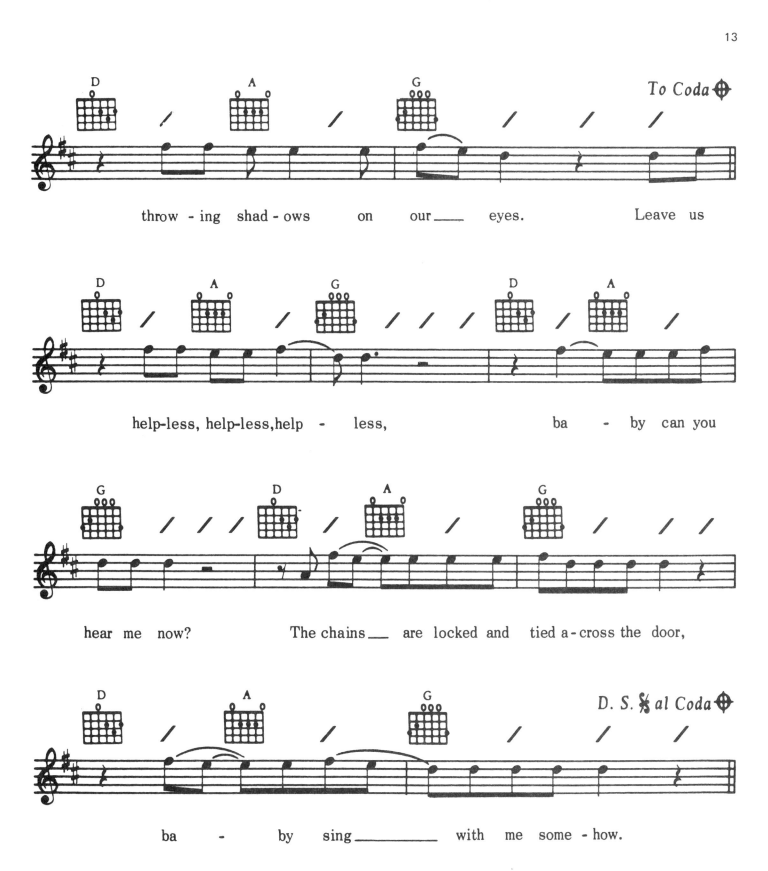

To Coda ⊕

throw - ing shad - ows on our___ eyes. Leave us

help-less, help-less, help - less, ba - by can you

hear me now? The chains___ are locked and tied a-cross the door,

D. S. 𝄋 al Coda ⊕

ba - by sing_____ with me some - how.

Coda ⊕ *Repeat and fade*

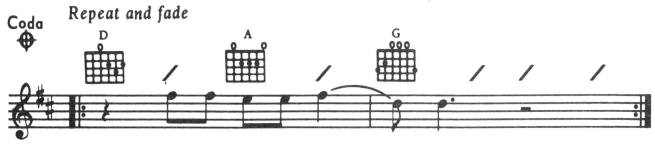

help - less, help-less, help - less.

COWGIRL IN THE SAND

Words and Music by
NEIL YOUNG

HARVEST

Words and Music by
NEIL YOUNG

Moderate Country style

1. Did I see you down in a young girl's town with your moth-er in so much pain? I was al-most there at the top of the stairs with her scream-in' in the rain. Did she wake you up to tell you that it was on-ly a change of plan? Dream up, dream up, let me fill your cup with the prom-ise of a man.

2. Did I

2. Did I see you walking with the boys, though it was not hand in hand?
And was some black face in a lonely place when you could understand?
Did she wake you up *(etc.)*

3. Will I see you give more than I can take; will I only harvest some?
As the days fly past will we lose our grasp or fuse it in the sun?
Did she wake you up *(etc.)*

COMES A TIME

Words and Music by
NEIL YOUNG

Oh, _____ this old world _____ keeps _

spin - nin' 'round. _____ It's a won - der tall

trees ain't _ lay - in' down. _____ There comes a time. _____

1.
(guitar)

2.
There comes a

Repeat and fade
(guitar)

time. _____
There comes a

Don't Let It Bring You Down

Words and Music by
NEIL YOUNG

Slowly, in 2

Old man ly - in' by the side of the road___ with the
Blind man run - ning through the light of the night___ with an

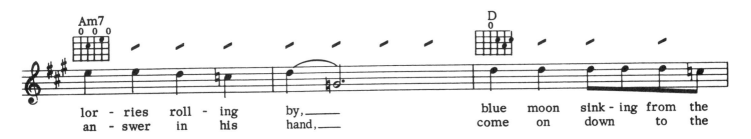

lor - ries roll - ing by,_____ blue moon sink - ing from the
an - swer in his hand,_____ come on down to the

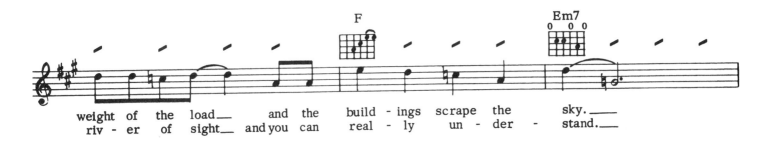

weight of the load___ and the build - ings scrape the sky.___
riv - er of sight___ and you can real - ly un - der - stand.___

Cold wind rip - ping down the al - ley at dawn___ and the morn - ing pa - per
Red lights flash - ing through the win - dow in the rain, can you hear the si - rens

flies, ___ dead man ly - ing by the side of the road___ with the
moan? ___ White cane ly - ing in a gut - ter in the lane if you're

GOIN' BACK

Words and Music by
NEIL YOUNG

Slowly, in 2

1. In a for - eign land, — there were crea-

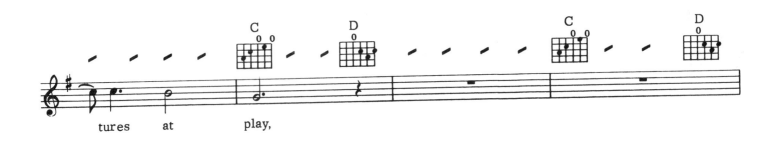

tures at play,

run-ning hand — in hand, — need-ing no -

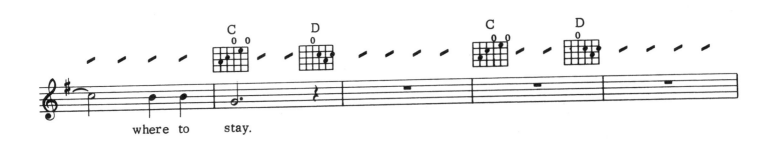

where to stay.

Driv-en to the moun-tains high, — they were sunk-en in the

Additional lyrics

2. I feel like going back, back where there's nowhere to stay.
   When fire filled the sky, I still remember that day.
   These rocks I'm climbing down, have already left the ground,
   Careening through space.

3. I used to build these buildings; I used to walk next to you.
   Their shadows tore us apart, and now we do what we do,
   Driven to the mountains high, sunken in the cities deep,
   Living in our sleep.

THE LONER

Words and Music by
NEIL YOUNG

Chorus

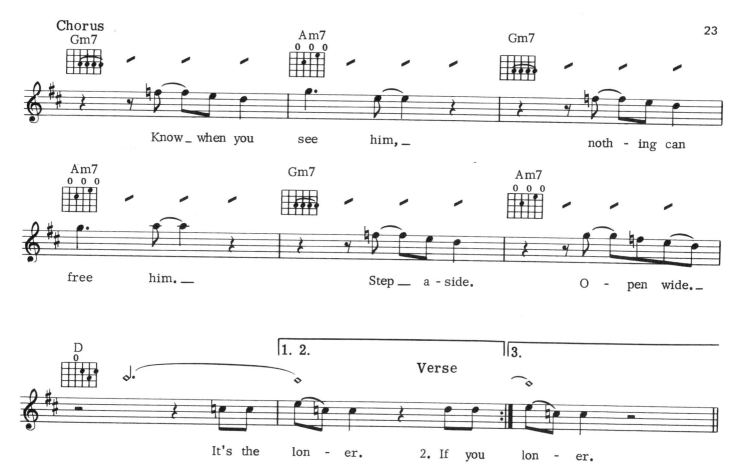

Know_ when you see him, _ noth - ing can

free him. _ Step _ a - side. O - pen wide. _

Verse

It's the lon - er. 2. If you lon - er.

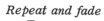

Repeat and fade

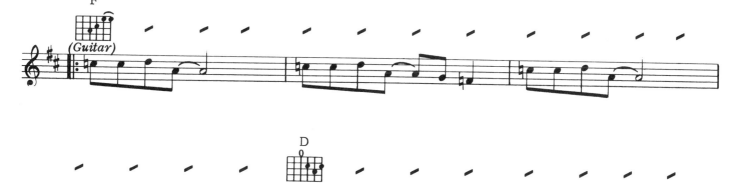

(Guitar)

Additional lyrics

2. If you see him in the subway, he'll be down at the end of the car,
Watching you move until he knows he knows who you are.
When you get off at your station alone, he'll know that you are.

(Chorus)

3. There was a woman he knew about a year or so ago.
She had something that he needed and he pleaded with her not to go.
On the day that she left, he died, but it did not show.

(Chorus)

THE NEEDLE AND THE DAMAGE DONE

Words and Music by
NEIL YOUNG

BIRDS

Words and Music by
NEIL YOUNG

HEART OF GOLD

Words and Music by
NEIL YOUNG

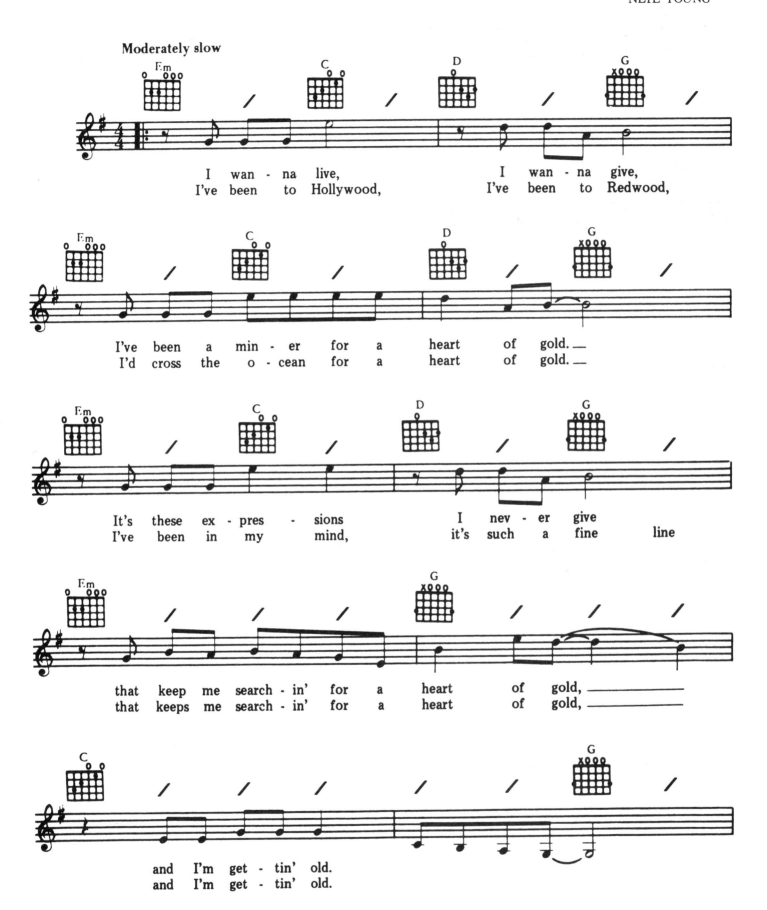

27

Keep me search-in' for a heart of gold, _____
Keeps me search-in' for a heart of gold, _____

and I'm get-tin' old.
and I'm get-tin' old.

Keep me search-in' for a heart of gold, __

you keep me search-in' and I'm grow-in' old. ____

Keep me search-in' for a heart of gold, __ I've been a min-er for a

heart of gold. _____

OLD MAN

Words and Music by
NEIL YOUNG

29

PEACE OF MIND

Words and Music by
NEIL YOUNG

ALABAMA

Words and Music by
NEIL YOUNG

HERE WE ARE IN THE YEARS

Words and Music by
NEIL YOUNG

HOLD BACK THE TEARS

Words and Music by
NEIL YOUNG

Additional lyrics

Two lying fools, and then four crying eyes,
Counting on one another to survive.
Crazy love must surely have this pain
If getting it up means going down again.
Hold back the tears *(etc.)*

JOURNEY THRU THE PAST

Words and Music by
NEIL YOUNG

Moderately slow

1. When the win - ter rains come pour - in' down on
go - in' back to Can - a - da on a

that new home of mine, will you think of me and
jour - ney through the past, and I won't be back till

won - der if I'm fine?
Feb - ru - ar - y comes.

Will your
"I will

rest - less heart come back to mine on a jour - ney through the
stay with you if you'll stay with me," said the fid - dler to the

past?
drum,

Will I still be in your eyes and on your
and we'll keep good time on a jour - ney through the

LOTTA LOVE

Words and Music by
NEIL YOUNG

I BELIEVE IN YOU

Words and Music by
NEIL YOUNG

Now that you've found_ your-self los-ing your mind,_are you here_ a-gain,
Com-ing to you_ at night I see_ my ques-tions, I feel_ my_ doubts,

find-ing that what_ you once thought was real_ is gone_ and chang-ing?
wish-ing that may-be in a year or two_ we could laugh_ and let it all out.

Now that you made_ your-self love me, do you think I can change_ it in a day?

How can I place_ you a-bove me? Am I ly-ing to you_ when I say

that I be-lieve in you?_ Oh, oh,_ oh, oh,_

oh, oh,_ I be-lieve in you._

1. D(hold)
2. D(hold)

A MAN NEEDS A MAID

Words and Music by
NEIL YOUNG

Moderately slow

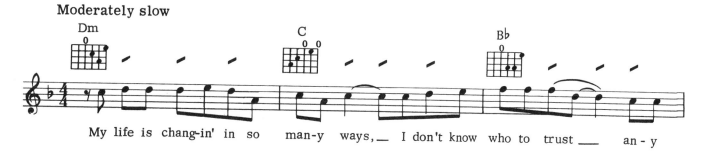

My life is chang-in' in so man-y ways, __ I don't know who to trust __ an - y

more.   There's a sha-dow run-nin' through my days   like a

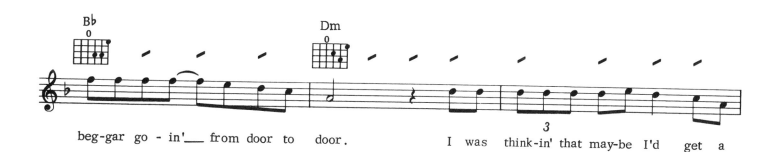

beg-gar go - in' __ from door to door.   I was think-in' that may-be I'd get a

maid,   find a   place near - by __ for her to   stay.

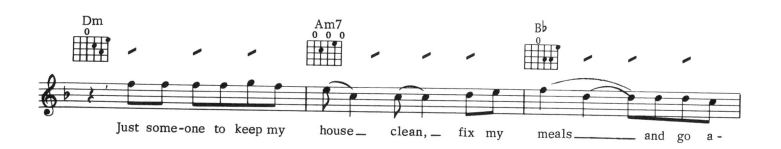

Just some-one to keep my   house __ clean, __ fix my   meals _____ and go a-

44

CINNAMON GIRL

Words and Music by
NEIL YOUNG

TELL ME WHY

Words and Music by
NEIL YOUNG

OHIO

Words and Music by
NEIL YOUNG

Moderate March tempo

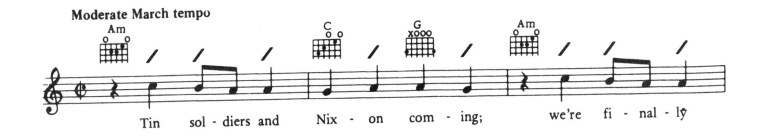

Tin sol-diers and Nix-on com-ing; we're fi-nal-ly

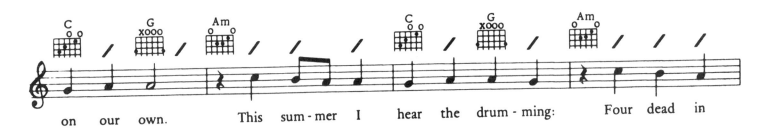

on our own. This sum-mer I hear the drum-ming: Four dead in

To Coda

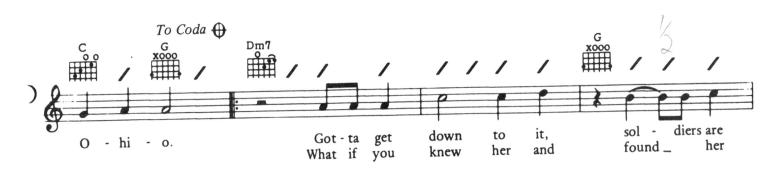

O - hi - o.

Got-ta get down to it, sol-diers are
What if you knew her and found __ her

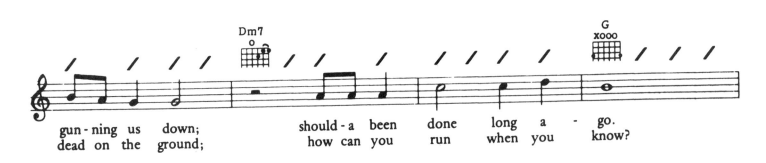

gun-ning us down; should-a been done long a - go.
dead on the ground; how can you run when you know?

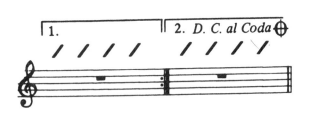

Repeat and fade

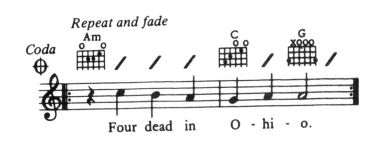

Four dead in O - hi - o.

Human Highway

Words and Music by
NEIL YOUNG

Moderately, in 2

1..I come down from the mist - y moun - tain.
down from the crook - ed man - sion.

I got lost on the hu-man high - way.
I went lookin' for the D. J.'s daugh - ter.

Take my head, re - fresh-ing foun - tain.
Since that day, I heard it men-tioned

Take my eyes from what they've seen. Take my
that my name is on the line. Now my

head _____ and change my mind
name _____ is on the line. } How could peo-

ple get so un - kind? _____

2. I come

EVERYBODY KNOWS THIS IS NOWHERE

Words and Music by
NEIL YOUNG

Moderate Country style

I think I'd like to go___ back home___ and take it
Ev-'ry time I think about back home___ it's cool and

eas - y.
breez - y. There's a wom- an that I'd like to get to know___
I wish that I could be___ there right now,___

a - liv-ing there.
just pass-ing time. } Ev-'ry-bod-y seems to

won - der_____ what it's like down__ here._____ I

got - ta get a - way from this day-to-day run-nin' a - round. Ev-'ry-bod-y

knows this is no - where. La la la la la la la.

Ev-'ry-bod-y, ev-'ry-bod-y knows.__ La la la la la la la.____

Repeat and fade

La la la la la la la.____

On THE WAY HOME

Words and Music by
NEIL YOUNG

LIKE A HURRICANE

Words and Music by
NEIL YOUNG

Chorus

You are like a hur-ri-cane: There's calm in your eye.__

And I'm get-ting blown__ a-way. There's some-where saf-er where the

feel-ings stay.__ I wan-na love you but I'm get-ting blown a-way.__

(guitar)

1. 2.

3.

Additional lyric

3. You are just a dreamer and I am just a dream,
And you could have been anyone to me.
Before that moment you touched my lips,
That perfect feeling when time just slips away between us
and our foggy trips.

Chorus

MOTORCYCLE MAMA

Words and Music by
NEIL YOUNG

Moderately

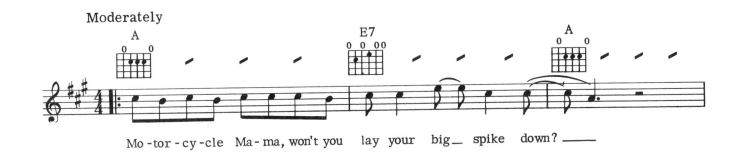

Mo-tor-cy-cle Ma-ma, won't you lay your big__ spike down? ___

Mo-tor-cy-cle Ma-ma, won't you lay your big __ spike down?_

___ I al-ways get in trou-ble when you

bring it a-round.__ Mo-tor-cy-cle Ma-ma, won't you lay it down?

To Coda ⊕

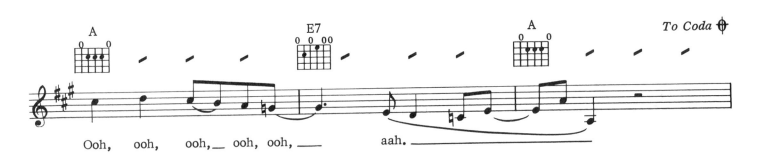

Ooh, ooh, ooh,__ ooh, ooh, ___ aah. _____

OUT ON THE WEEKEND

Words and Music by
NEIL YOUNG

Moderately slow

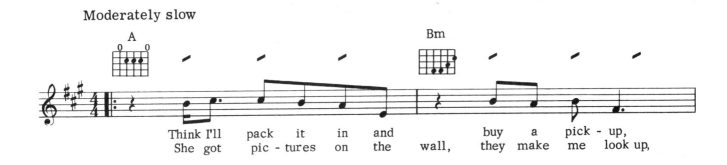

Think I'll pack it in and buy a pick - up,
She got pic - tures on the wall, they make me look up,

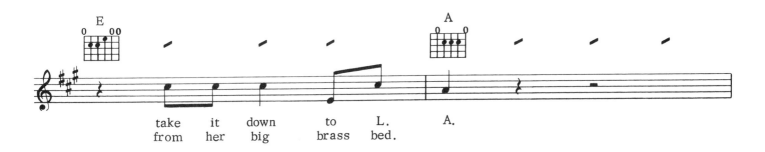

take it down to L. A.
from her big brass bed.

Find a place to call my own and try to fix up,
Now I'm run - nin' down the road try - in' to stay up,

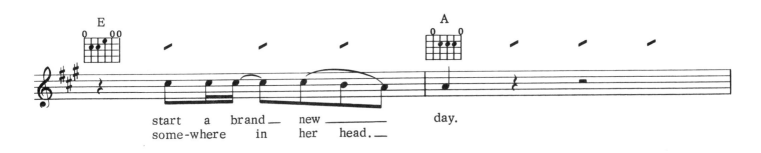

start a brand new day.
some - where in her head.

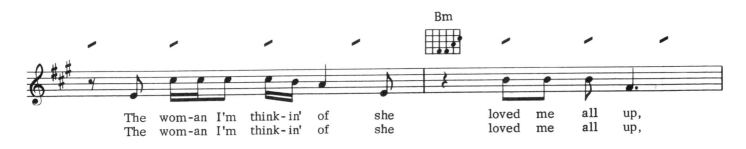

The wom - an I'm think - in' of she loved me all up,
The wom - an I'm think - in' of she loved me all up,

ROUND AND ROUND AND ROUND

Words and Music by
NEIL YOUNG

hard e-nough los-in' the pa-per il-lu-sion you've hid-den in-

side with-out the con-fu-sion of find-in' you're

us-in' the crutch of the lie to

shel-ter your pride when you cry.

D. C. (play through Chorus) and fade on Instrumental Verse

cries.

Additional lyrics

(Chorus)

2. Now you're movin' too slow, and wherever you go there's another besides.
It's so hard to say no to yourself, and it shows that you're losing inside
When you step on your pride and you cry.

(Chorus)

3. How the hours will bend through the time that you spend till you turn to your eyes
And you see your best friend looking over the end, and you turn to see why,
And he looks in your eyes and he cries.

(Chorus)

4. *Instrumental (fade)*

(WHEN YOU'RE ON) THE LOSING END

Words and Music by
NEIL YOUNG

hard   for   me   now,   but   I'll   make   it   some -

how, _ though I know   I'll nev-er be the same.   Won't you

ev - er change your ways?   It's so hard   to make love

pay   when you're   on   the los - ing   end. ___

And   I'll   feel   that way a - gain. _____

Well, I

WHAT DID YOU DO TO MY LIFE?

Words and Music by
NEIL YOUNG

WORDS

Words and Music by
NEIL YOUNG

Slowly

Am · F · G

1. Some-one and some-one were down by the pond, — look-in' for some-thin' to
I was a junk-man sell-in' you cars, — wash-in' your win - dows and

Am · F

plant - in the lawn. — Out in the fields — they were turn-in' the soil, — I'm
shin - in' your stars. — Think-in' your mind — was my own in a dream, —

G · Am

sit - tin' here hop - in' this wa - ter will boil. — When I look through the win - dow and
what would you won - der, and how would it seem? — Liv - in' in - tles a

F · G · Am

out on the road, — they're bring-in' me pres - ents and say - in' hel - lo, — sing-in'
bit at a time, — the king start-ed laugh - in' and talk - in' in rhyme, - sing-in' }

Am · F · G · Am

words, words, — be-tween the lines of age. — Words,

F · G · 1. Am · 2. Am

words, — be-tween the lines of age. — 2. If —

TILL THE MORNING COMES

Words and Music by
NEIL YOUNG

CRIPPLE CREEK FERRY

Words and Music by
NEIL YOUNG

ALREADY ONE

Words and Music by
NEIL YOUNG

Additional lyrics

2. Your laughing eyes, your crazy smile,
   Every time I look in his face.
   I can't believe how love lasts a while
   And looks like forever in the first place.

   (Chorus)

3. In my new life, I'm traveling light,
   Eyes wide open for the next move.
   I can't go wrong till I get right,
   But I'm not falling back in the same groove.

   (Chorus)

DON'T BE DENIED

Words and Music by
NEIL YOUNG

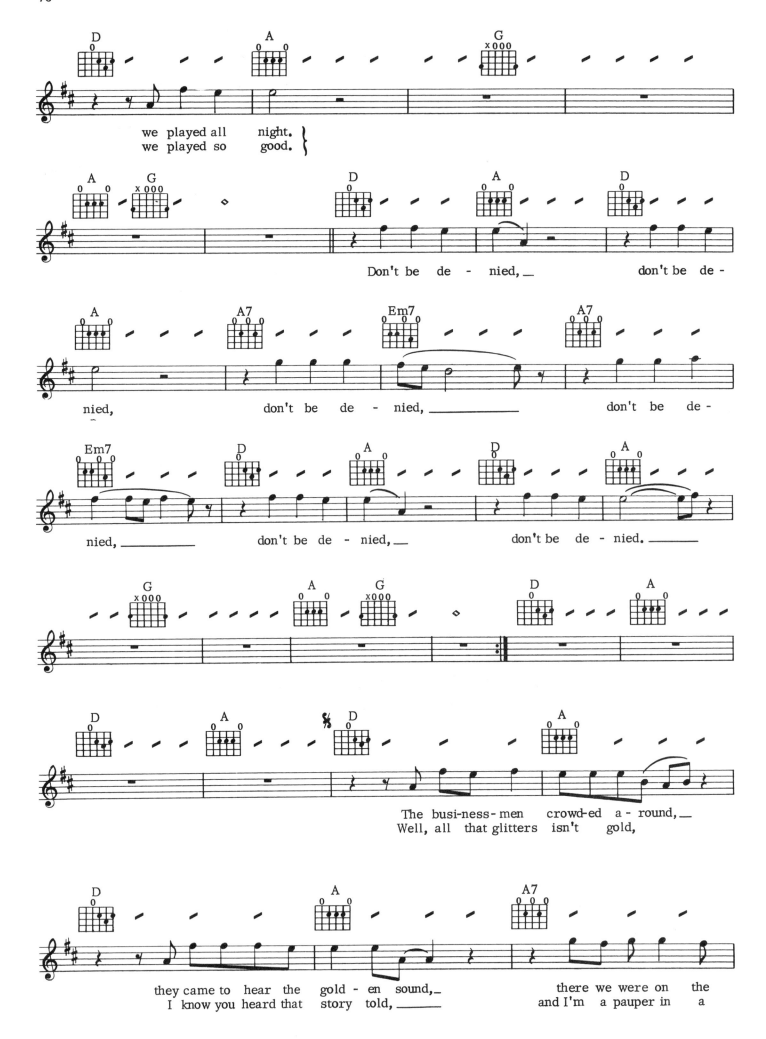

71

OLD COUNTRY WALTZ

Words and Music by
NEIL YOUNG

Moderate Country Waltz

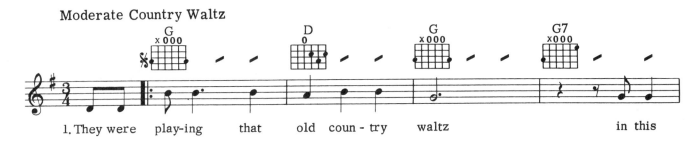

1. They were play-ing that old coun-try waltz in this

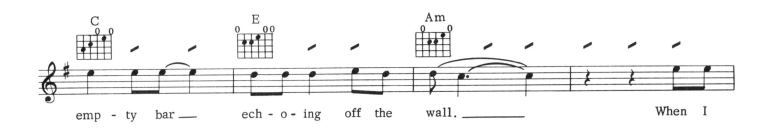

emp-ty bar ech-o-ing off the wall. When I

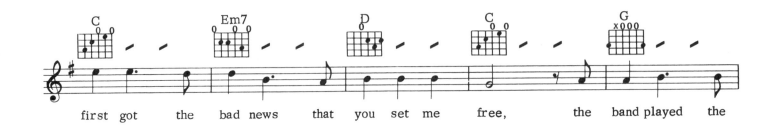

first got the bad news that you set me free, the band played the

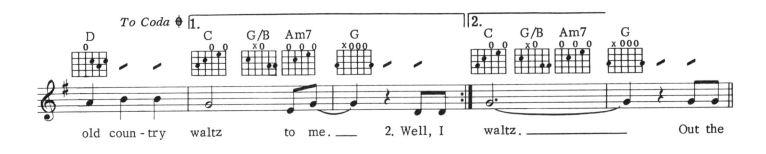

old coun-try waltz to me. 2. Well, I waltz. Out the

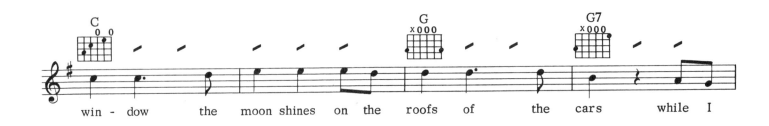

win-dow the moon shines on the roofs of the cars while I

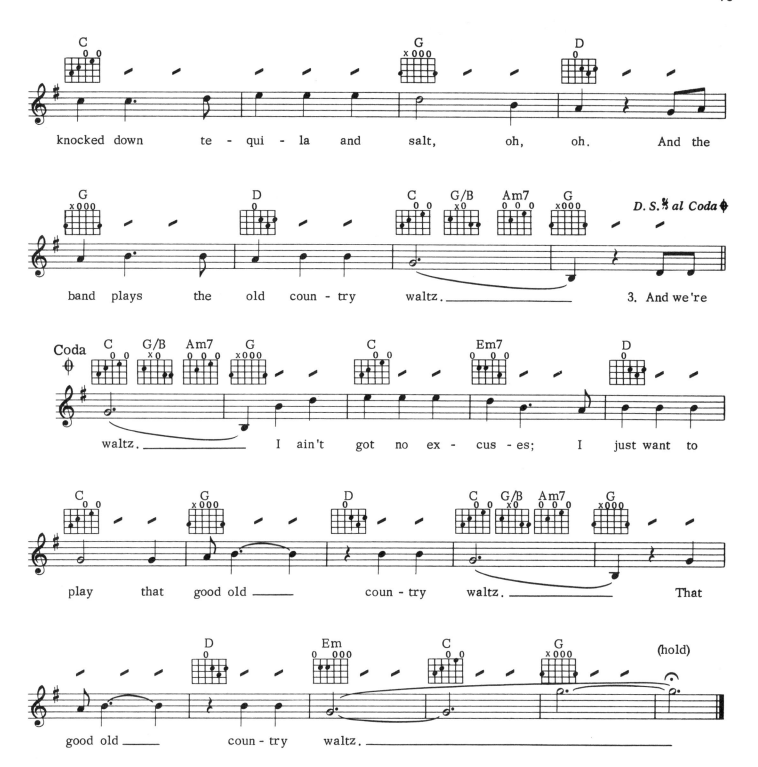

Additional lyrics

2. Well, I loved, I lost, and I cried
   The day that the two of us died.
   Ain't got no excuses; I just want to ride
   While the band plays the old country waltz.
   Out the window *(etc.)*

3. And we're playing it, that old country waltz
   In this empty bar echoing off the wall.
   Ain't got no excuses; we just want to play
   That good old country waltz.
   I ain't got no excuses *(etc.)*

I'VE LOVED HER SO LONG

Words and Music by
NEIL YOUNG

She's a vic - tim of her sens - es; do you know her? Can you

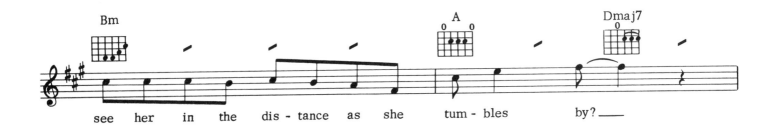

see her in the dis - tance as she tum - bles by? ___

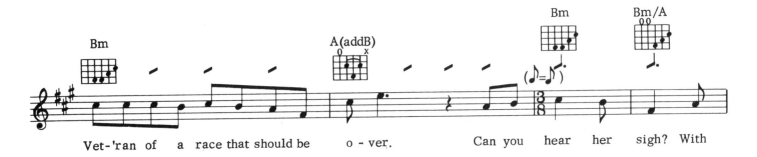

Vet-'ran of a race that should be o - ver. Can you hear her sigh? With

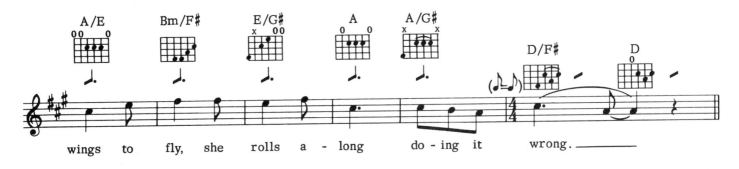

wings to fly, she rolls a - long do - ing it wrong. ___

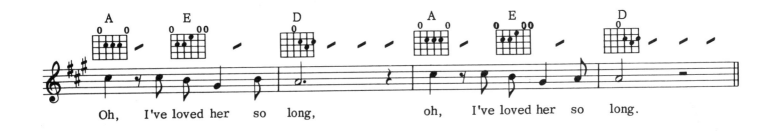

Oh, I've loved her so long, oh, I've loved her so long.

WALK ON

Words and Music by
NEIL YOUNG

Moderately

I hear some peo - ple been ___ talk - in' me ___
I re mem - ber the ___ good old days,—

___ down, bring up my name,
stayed up all night

pass it 'round. They don't men - tion the
get - tin' crazed. Then the mon - ey was

hap - py times; they do
not so good, but do we

their thing, ___ I'll do mine.
still did the best we could.

Oo, ba - by, that's hard to change;—

77

DO I HAVE TO COME RIGHT OUT AND SAY IT?

Words and Music by
NEIL YOUNG

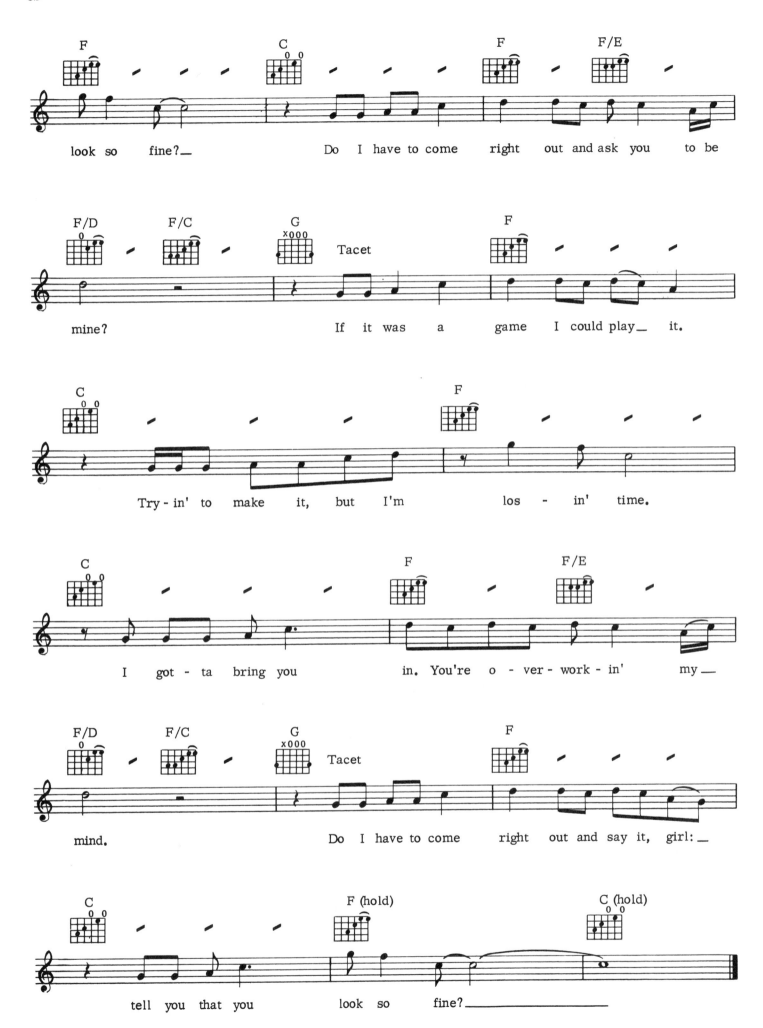

STAR OF BETHLEHEM

Words and Music by
NEIL YOUNG

Moderate Country style

1. Ain't it hard when you wake up in the morn-ing, and you
dreams and your lov-ers won't pro-tect you; they're

find out that those oth-er days are gone? All you have _ is
on-ly pass-ing through you in the end. They'll leave you stripped-of

mem-o-ries _ of hap-pi-ness _ lin-ger - in' _
all that they _ can get to, and wait for you to come back a -

on. _____
gain. _____

1. 2.   3.

(hold)

2. All your
3. Yet

Additional lyrics

3. Yet still a light is shining from that lamp on down the hall.
Maybe the star of Bethlehem wasn't a star at all.

HEY BABE!

Words and Music by
NEIL YOUNG

TIME FADES AWAY

Words and Music by
NEIL YOUNG

Additional lyrics

2. Back in Canada, I spend my days,
   Riding subways through a haze.
   I was handcuffed, I was born and raised.

   (Chorus)

3. Thirteen junkies too weak to work,
   One sells diamonds for what they're worth.
   Down on pain street disappointment lurks.

   (Chorus)

SADDLE UP THE PALOMINO

Words by
NEIL YOUNG, TIM DRUMMOND
and BOBBY CHARLES

Music by
NEIL YOUNG

Additional lyrics

2. If you can't cut it, don't pick up the knife.
There's no reward in your conscience stored
When you're sleepin' with another man's wife.

(Chorus)

3. I wanna lick the platter; the gravy doesn't matter.
It's a cold bowl of chili when love lets you down,
But it's the neighbor's wife I'm after.

(Chorus)

SEA OF MADNESS

Words and Music by
NEIL YOUNG

Moderate Rock beat

How can I bring you to this sea___ of mad - ness? I
I went to heav - en and I stood at the cross - roads, I'll

love you so much___ it's gon - na bring me sad - ness.
love you to - mor - row as sure as the wind blows.

I've nev - er seen it through these eyes___ be - fore,___ now I
Sil - ver rain___ on the moun - tain clo - ver

don't be - lieve it,___ I think I'll take it or leave_ it.
wash-es a - way_ un - til the mu - sic is o - ver. } All I need is your

sweet, sweet lov - in'; fill my life with hap - pi - ness. All I want is your

heart; ev - 'ry time I think of you, mine falls a - part.

SUGAR MOUNTAIN

Words and Music by
NEIL YOUNG

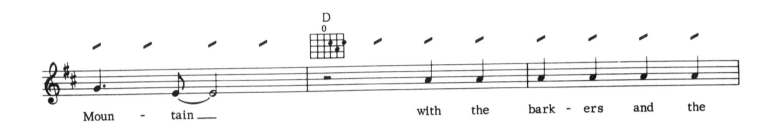

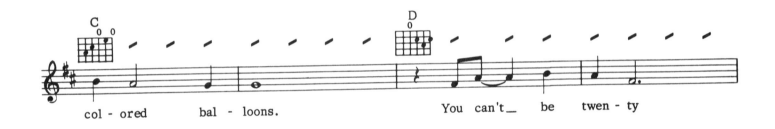

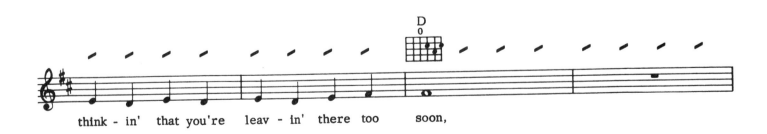

you're leav - in' there too soon.

Verse

1. It's so nois - y at the fair, but all your friends are there. And the can - dy floss you had, and your moth - er and your dad.

soon.

(Chorus)

2. There's a girl just down the aisle,
Oh, to turn and see her smile.
You can hear the words she wrote
As you read the hidden note.

(Chorus)

3. Now you're underneath the stairs
And you're givin' back some glares
To the people who you met,
And it's your first cigarette.

(Chorus)

4. Now you say you're leavin' home
'Cause you want to be alone,
Ain't it funny how you feel
When you're findin' out it's real.

(Chorus)

AFTER THE GOLD RUSH

Words and Music by
NEIL YOUNG

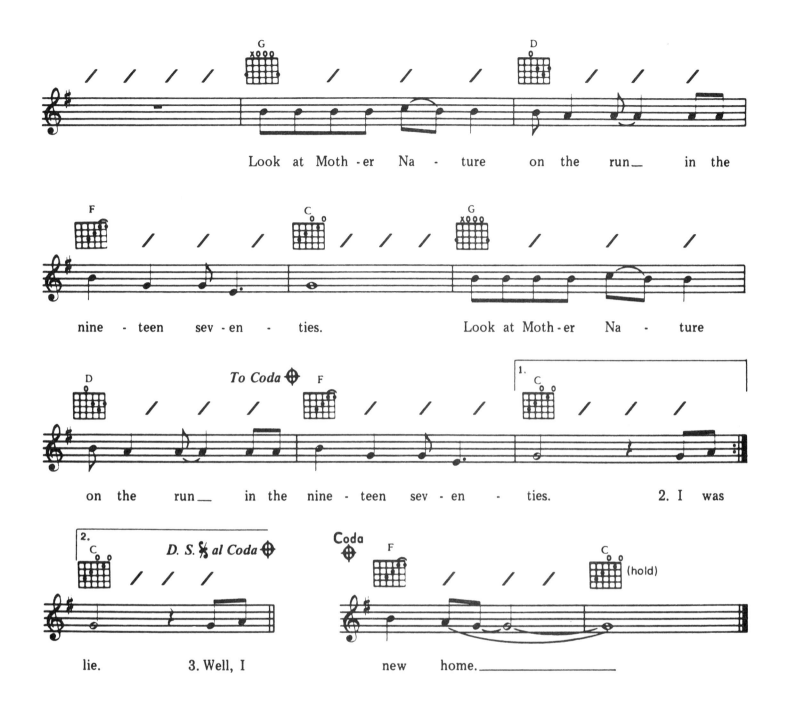

2. I was lyin' in a burned-out basement with the full moon in my eyes.
I was hopin' for replacement when the sun burst through the sky.
There was a band playin' in my head and I felt like getting high.
I was thinkin' about what a friend had said, I was hopin' it was a lie.
Thinkin' about what a friend had said, I was hopin' it was a lie.

3. Well, I dreamed I saw the silver spaceships flyin' in the yellow haze of the sun.
There were children cryin' and colors flyin' all around the chosen ones.
All in a dream, all in a dream, the loading had begun.
Flying Mother Nature's silver seed to a new home in the sun.
Flying Mother Nature's silver seed to a new home.

SOUTHERN MAN

Words and Music by
NEIL YOUNG

LOVE IS A ROSE

Words and Music by
NEIL YOUNG

ONLY LOVE CAN BREAK YOUR HEART

Words and Music by
NEIL YOUNG